REDEFINING BLACK AND CORRECTING HIS-STORY

RAY STONE

Ra One Publications LLC

Redefining Black & Correcting His-Story.

Copyright © 2019 by Ray Stone

Manufactured in the US Republic (Northwest Amexem)

10 9 8 7 6 5 4 3 2 1

For Library of Congress Data, See Publisher

E-mail: **rstone.el@icloud.com**

Web: www.ra1books.com

Phone: (313) 355-3949

Take advantage of our unique services including:

* Speaking Engagements * Detox Consultations

* Office Lunch Visits * Kitchen/Bathroom Makeovers

Design & Layout: https://www.jschlenker.com/

Editing: Rashid El

Photo Credits: Various Sources

Contents

Message to the Reader

Peace and love,

The purpose of this book is to spread new information and raise questions. Any actions taken as a result of this information are the sole responsibility of the reader, the author nor publisher cannot be held responsible in any way. If you plan to get involved with changing your records and status legally, be very meticulous. Do your homework and make sure that you know what you're doing. It is not a game.

We hope that this book motivates you to do some light research of your own. It's so important that you talk with your elders in your family while you can, learn more about your own ancestry. Trace your roots back as far as you can. Pass that valuable information down to future generations, don't let your history be forgotten.

Always give honor and thanks to your ancestors who came before you. Thanks for reading.

Nipsey Hussle was exactly the type of proactive and intelligent dude that I wanted to have a copy of this book.

And to my lil brother Doogie,
Andre Coles.
R.I.P.

I am light…
I am not the color of my eyes
I am not the skin
on the outside
I am not my age
I am not my race
My soul inside is all light, all light.

~ I am light by **India Arie**

White Jesus

T his long trip down the rabbit hole started for me with the white Jesus. When I was growing up, the majority of my friends in my neighborhood and family members had a picture of white Jesus in their home. All the Bible characters in pics, books, and in movies always looked like this:

It never made any sense to me. How could everyone have that pale skin? It was hot enough for them to be barefoot, with green grass and blue skies —so wouldn't they at least be tanned?

At my mom's church, other than the politicians who sat uncomfortably through services during election time, there was nothing but black members. The highly admired Bishop was very dark complected with skin like burnt brass. However the most prominent picture in the building was the one of a white Jesus hanging high over our heads.

I would stare at the large image as I daydreamed

through the seemingly endless church services. Sunday after Sunday, I never understood how a congregation full of black people were singing, dancing, and praising under this white guy. How did this happen?

Black people are very spiritual, and our families are generally serious about religion. We believe in and rely on the power of prayer. Praying to a white Jesus can tacitly give our people an inferior complex. The irony of it was not lost on me as a youth, it bothered me incessantly.

Whenever I asked about why he was white, people would say that it doesn't matter what color he was—they'd say I should not be distracted by that image, or it was just the devil trying to distract me from having a relationship with Jesus. Their reasoning was that God is a spirit and actually had no color, but all the images I saw of Jesus definitely had a color—it was that pale white dude.

If the image of the main character doesn't matter either way, then why not just have a Savior that looks more like us, who we could better relate to? Those questions never got answered.

As an adult, I eventually learned exactly how Christianity was forced upon civilizations via ugly wars and evil crusades. People were publicly tortured and murdered in mass while being coerced into accepting Jesus Christ as their personal lord and savior. That's the real reason that the image of Jesus is ubiquitous.

When I heard about that Bible verse (Revelation 1:15), that said he had wooly hair and skin like burnt brass, I was stoked. I figured that it would alter the image of Jesus forever, at least for black folks. It didn't. The white Jesus pic was already cemented.

Go to YouTube and search for 'Good Times white Jesus.' The youngest son Micheal had replaced the white Jesus hanging in the Evans family home with a black Jesus. His mom, Florida, had a fit. She explained that she had a deep attachment to that white Jesus. "When I was baby I don't know what I saw first," she said, "my mamma, my poppa, or this Jesus, now he's the one I know and love."

That's basically how it went for all of us, we've only known one image of Jesus in our lifetime. I don't know if it's because I've grown far away from the church world or if I've made myself blind to it, but I hardly ever see that image anymore. It used to haunt me everywhere. Looking at it in this book brought back lots of memories from my childhood.

In those days I was a lot more militant. I would tune out anyone who I thought wasn't about a revolution. Everything was black or white to me at that time, and I was on my black power stuff. Since then I've grown so much more patient and wise. I realize that this system and our pcople's issues are not as simple as black or white. It's a deeper game thats being played and we have to zoom out and see the bigger picture in order to win.

Dear Black People

The first thing that needs to be fully understood about Black history is that in the past there was no such thing as black people. Historically, people were never referred to or categorized by color or skin complexion. *Things* are categorized in colors, not people. There can be a black car, or black sweater —but not a black person.

There have been several changes in the labels used to describe our people. That was done in order to keep us confused about our true identities. Just in the last hundred years alone, us "blacks" have answered to several different brand names. It went from **Negro**, to **colored**, to **Afro-American**, until today where the politically accepted terms for us are **black** or **African-Americans**.

Those names were brands given to our people during and after subjugation, it's not what we historically called ourselves. Today although it's hard, we have to learn to completely disassociate from the terms that we've been using to identify ourselves.

Black history is technically very short, hell, I see why it's in February. That name has only existed since 1850. As people of color, we already know that our lineage and roots trace all the way back to the origin of humanity. It's the terminology that we use which disconnects us from our expansive history.

In school they've always taught us that we were severed from our history during the slave trade. In that narrative we were all kidnapped from our home and brought to this new, foreign land. That's a misnomer that is taught and reinforced on purpose.

The powers that be don't want us to make the connection to our royal history and legacy. They want us to accept the notion that our American history began with slavery; schools teach us that because 'they' made up the curriculum. Ample evidence shows that people of color have been in the Americas long before any European arrival. The same "black" people who look just like the who you would see in any hood in America right now were always here. It's always been our hood.

So a good question is what **were our people called before 1492?** Better yet, what were we calling ourselves back then?

Before even discussing the answer, we should establish the fact that we do have a history in the Americas that far predates slavery. We've had indigenous civilizations not only all over the Americas, but all over the globe.

Africa is the most mineral rich land on the earth. It is the Motherland. If we knew the massive extent of our history, we'd recognize that everywhere is our home. America is our great Auntie; this land is not new like school leads us to believe, it's ancient also. American history courses purposely skew our scope of the past.

3

Follow the Etymology

E tymology = the study of the history of words, roots, and stems and how they change over time.

[From the Greek **etymon** (true sense) + logia (study of) = study of true sense.]

THE TRUTH CAN BE hard to uncover in the United States. The English language itself is built for deception as it's full of words with duplicitous meanings. There are over a million words in English, far more than any other language. Developing a vast vocabulary and understanding of the etymology words is an essential component of research.

Learning what words historically meant and where they came from can help understand what was happening in that time period.

As we already established, the names Indian, Afro-American, African-American, Negro, Nigger, and black are all labels placed on us since 1492—they're not historical terms.

We should begin our search looking into older dictionaries because the newer revisions have omitted or truncated some of the definitions. The 1828 Webster's Dictionary has the following description of American:

AMER'ICAN, noun A native of America; **originally applied to the aboriginals, or copper-colored races, found here** by the Europeans; but now applied to the descendants of Europeans born in America.

That definition alone should tell us that we were already here in this land. It says it right there. We were not defined as "black" at that time, we were copper-colored, just like we still are today. People of color are natives in the Americas too.

Also, note that the definition of American mentions copper colored races—plural—indicating that there were several races and tribes of copper-colored Americans here; not just one. You can hold a penny up to yourself and recognize that you are in your homeland right now.

We get a picture in our head of Native Americans with a stereotypical look, with long straight hair. They control the imagery just like they did with Jesus. Today "black" people hear the term American Indian and think of someone that doesn't look like us, but that is a misnomer.

In fact, we can see that we are one and the same from the Oxford Dictionary's third definition for the word **nigger**:

nigger

3 a. A dark-skinned person of any origin. *__In early U.S. use usually with reference to American Indians__*. Usually offensive.

Wow. So American Indians were once called niggers, just like us, because we are the same people and just don't realize it. Think about it, doesn't every 'black' person know or say something about having some '*Indian*' somewhere in their family? Yes. Because we all do.

The term American is *now* applied to Europeans born in America. They've morphed themselves into the Americans, while the real aboriginals keep getting called all these different names. How does this make any sense? The further you go down this rabbit hole, you will understand how the facts were hidden so the land could be taken from its original inhabitants.

One thing revealed in studying history is that the pen is far mightier than the sword. Reclassifying people and reconstructing history allowed for them to redefine the American. Once people agree to call themselves a color, then codes and colorable laws were made to govern this new classification of persons. Now they are legally able to treat us like subjects in our own home.

And again, by calling this home it's not disparaging Africa in any way at all. We are proud of our African heritage as well, but we should know that we don't have to cross the ocean to find our history. Make sure that you understand that just like we had great empires there, we had great empires in the Americas too. Just like there are pyramids in Egypt, there are pyramids in the Americas and other parts of the world also. Our ancestors were skilled sailors and navigators of the sea and had traveled all over the world many times.

In fact, you can look elsewhere to find your

history. Everywhere on the planet, there is definitive evidence of the presence of people of color, or so-called black people. We will look at some examples of that in forthcoming chapters.

4

The Transatlantic Slave Trade

We all know the early lessons of education teach us that African people were stolen in mass and brought to America.

The horror of slavery and the slave trade is well documented in American history. It's basically all they teach us about black people in school. Every few years Hollywood makes a movie or two featuring slaves and masters. Slavery and racism are continually being reinforced in American news and media.

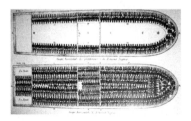

When I think about it, the images on either side of this paragraph are the main things that come to my mind when I think about slavery. One is the diagram of the slave ship which is the most prominent image of slavery. Then there is the picture with the man with the huge welts on his back. How many times have we seen those same images? Countless. They are ingrained into our heads by now.

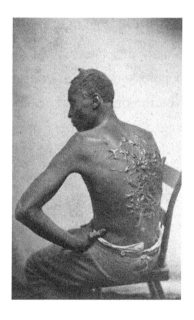

There is a great disparity when it comes to talking about the number of people involved in the Transatlantic slave trade. The numbers are never consistent with some older sources claiming that over one hundred million people were brought from Africa to the Americas.

The most recent number that seems to be agreed upon is 12.5 million. The slave years are listed from 1619–1858. For that to add up, it would mean ninety voyages per year, for 366 years straight. That means every four days, year-round across the very brutal Atlantic Ocean, there would have to be a ship arriving with at least 380 living slaves aboard.

People believe and accept it because it's written in the books and taught in schools. We act as if we don't know that our oppressors gave us education, religion, and history. Even the biggest slave ports do not have records of voyages with anywhere near that number of people.

Remember the ships were not massive like cruise ships, mostly small cargo boats were converted into slave boats. These were long journeys, (some say three to four months, others say between eight to eighteen months with necessary stops at various ports), where each person, even the slaves, would need fresh water daily to survive. How could there be room for all of those prisoners of war (slaves), plus water and food for such a long journey? Where did everyone use the bathroom? They told us that they just let them piss and defecate on each other under the decks, but no one could realistically survive that. And what about the storms and rough seasons? History scoffs at logical questions like that. Even our people sometimes get upset when questions are raised. How dare anyone dispute the details and disrespect our ancestors horrific suffering?

The critical component in stealing the land from the people was convincing us that we are not from here. The slave trade story and movies made us think that all 'black' people came from Africa, and that is not true at all. Many historians say that the slave trade is taught in reverse and that many enslaved people were actually shipped from America and taken to other parts of the world. Rewriting and creating a new history was a necessary evil. And we know that they have no problem telling lies. That's the reason that we have to question everything taught to us in schools, especially since they create the curriculum.

There were said to be as many as 66,000 slave ships, another inflated number. They would have to be powerful ships to withstand hundreds of thousands of trips back and forth across the rough Atlantic Ocean, overloaded with cargo. It's hard to imagine that there are not many preserved slave ships in museums. Where did all the ships go?

It seems as though Europeans would have a few

of them around like trophies. In fact, they love making slave period movies so much that Hollywood should build their own slave ship.

I once went to a museum exhibit featuring the tools of torture that were used during the Christian crusades. There were actual old handcuffs, guillotines, and other horrible medieval pieces of equipment that were used to publicly torture, maim, or kill the non-believers. It was gruesome, but they still have the actual tools. The crusades were from A.D. 1095–1230.

Museums have dinosaurs, mummies, and other ancient replicas and fossils from thousands of years ago. As horrible as it was, slavery is a huge part of American education. We can all imagine and describe the inhumane conditions of slave ships because we've been taught about it so much, yet there are none for us to see. The slave voyages reportedly lasted until 1867, which was not that long ago.

Challenging the slave trade with questions makes people assume that you are in denial about slavery. People think it's a case of not wanting to accept reality when it's just logical questions. They don't want us to think about it.

We've already accepted the slave trade story as fact many generations ago. Just like at some point in the past we thought it was a fact that Christopher Columbus discovered America. They tell us that's what happened in school, but later we find out that it's not true at all. America has set a precedent where we can't just accept anything taught to us. The rich people posing as philanthropists pumped money into education only to teach us what they wanted us to know. The quotes in this chapter speak to the ultimate goals of the public school system.

Slavery, religion, and education rely on the fact that people will not question anything. In fact, the goal of all of those institutions is to keep people mentally asleep. We owe it to ourselves and our ancestors to wake up and question everything.

"I don't want a nation of *thinkers*. I want a nation of **WORKERS**."

~ John D. Rockefeller

(Who invested unprecedented millions to implement a public schooling system, especially for the 'blacks' and underprivileged.)

"The aim of public education is **not** to spread enlightenment at all, it is simply to reduce as many individuals as possible to the same safe level, to breed and train a standardized citizenry, to put down dissent and originality."

~ H. L. Mencken

Some of our most brilliant scholars I know corroborate the slave trade story. Sometimes when someone is deeply rooted and credentialed academically, they can become impervious to any heterodox information. That is part of the educational process. Logistically, it's difficult to believe that 12.5 million people were transported from Africa to the Americas. Not only does it defy logic, there are also no records to support that slave trade involved anywhere near that number.

Much more evidence supports the idea that America was stolen from the people who were already here.

5

The US Census

The US Census first began in 1790. At that time there was no such classification as Indian or black as ethnic groups at all—it was only **free whites**, **free non-whites**, and **slaves**.

In the 1820s the Census had categories of **whites**, **coloreds**, and **slaves**. The "Indians" at that time were officially called colored people. Yes, just like so-called black people, because they are the same people.

It wasn't until the 1850 Census that the term black was introduced. The ethnic group choices then were **white**, **black**, or **mulatto**.

It was the 1860 Census when the term **Indian** was added. Before that time all the indigenous groups of people were either black, colored, or mulatto.

The visual of that version of history was mainly shaped by media and Hollywood imagery. We associate what a Native American looks like by the way Hollywood portrayed them. Dark skinned native people were purposely not depicted.

Remember that the original definition of American was the copper-colored RACES found here by the Europeans.

Crow Tribesman - 1873

The US Census in 1900 introduced what people call the **$5 dollar Indians**. All dark people, regardless if they were Indian or not, were listed as "black" on that census.

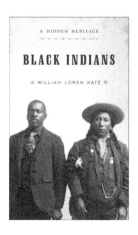

White Americans were able to classify themselves

as Indian on that census too if they paid the $5 fee to the Dawes Commission. After being told of the benefits that Indians were eligible for, many poor white families jumped on the bandwagon. The European opened the door for their own people to receive the things we were entitled to the aboriginals.

That helped to alter the image of an American Indian. We must understand that our ancestry is ancient, long before the Hollywood cowboys and Indians on horses. Horses were only brought to the Americas around the 16th or 17th Century. The Mound Builders and the other aboriginal tribes have roots here that are thousands of years before the modern image of an American Indians. We had been here.

6

Mother Africa

A frica is the Motherland.

This is a major point of dispute within today's conscious community. Since we have learned that we are at home and have roots in the Americas, our Pan-African family think that it is disparaging to Africa.

Here is where there is a big disconnect in our community. When some of us talk about being native to this land, there is an assumption that implies a denial of our African heritage.

It is not true. We still love Africa, I do at least.

Because of the deep emotional attachment we all have towards Africa, people don't want to hear anything about it not being our homeland. It needs to be understood that we can love and respect both cultures, as it's all one and the same anyway. We are the same people.

As a quick tangent, even way before any of my studies and life path took shape, I always used to think to myself at what point do you call a land your home? If your grandmother and her grandmother were born in a place where you are born, wouldn't that place be your home? I'd always thought that to be the case with us in America. You would love your family heritage of where the original mother was from (Africa), but would identify with your current location as your home.

Science says that all of humanity originates from Africa millions of years ago. People that we would describe as "black" people today have historical foot-prints all over the globe. Artifacts that we would call

"African" is found in India, Asia, Australia, Greenland—literally everywhere.

Pan Africanist will sometimes vehemently reject the notion of black people being "Indians." They suggest that the road to freedom and unity is to unite as Africans. Period. Many scholars, myself included, see things much differently.

Everyone pretty much agrees that the Olmecs were 'black,' 'Negroid,' or African people. Since they had posted up in the Americas long enough to build pyramids and giant stone statues, then this is obviously our homeland too!

The sculptures and monuments of the Olmec (pictured below), and Mayan cultures indicate highly developed civilizations. It had to take many generations, a great deal of organization, and masses of people to build structures of that magnitude. Some of the stone heads weigh as much as nine tons!

His-story says that the Olmecs were succeeded by the Mayan civilization, who eventually became extinct. Mysteriously. Remember that HIS-story is taught to us with a purpose. In all my years of school, I never saw any images like the one above. I would have never guessed that it was in the Americas. We were always taught that everything "black" was from Africa, but it is not true at all, it was contrived.

At that time in my mind, we were separate from Mexico. I didn't look at or embrace it as an actual part of the Americas when it is. Not only that, but our ancestors left so many markers there. An American upbringing tends to usher us have a separation with Mexico and Mexicans. That mentality continues with all this stupid 'build a wall' campaign. As I began to travel, I realize that there are tons of 'black' people all over this world. People assumed that I was Mexican and were speaking Spanish to me when I was in Mexico.

7

Pyramids

Pyramids are monuments that mark the existence of people of color. We mainly only know about the ones in Africa; however, there are many more. The squares on the map above mark the various places of the planet where pyramids can be found.

This proves that we so-called black people have lived all over the planet. As people profess their love for Africa, I try to explain to them that we are from everywhere. Our ancestors left timeless markers of their legacy, built with high-level Astrological science and mathematics, all over the world, including in the Americas.

8

Lies of His-Story

"Make the lie big, make it simple, keep saying it, and eventually they will believe it."

~ Adolf Hitler

The United States of America is a corporation that is built entirely on lies. The simple fact that Columbus is still credited with discovering America is one glaring example of that. They made the lie simple, the Indians were here, the Pilgrims came and took the land from them, and then brought in millions of slaves from Africa. That's basically how the story of American history is told.

The vast majority of people know and acknowledge

that this land was inhabited already, but still educational institutions credit Christopher Columbus with a discovery. That lie has been taught and repeated so much that it has become a fact and a nationally recognized holiday, even though most people know it's not true.

We should know by now that beyond the shadow of a doubt the powers that be in America will perpetuate lies. Some of the recent 'terrorist events' are manufactured for newscast as a scare tactic. Fake news. They've even lied about historic events like the moon landing or the attacks of 9/11, with no problem at all. It has become the American way. Distractions are kept in our faces while the 1% pull all of the strings. The people and entities who fund the schools decide what's in the textbooks.

The image that we have of native Americans is calculated. They never wanted 'black people' to associate ourselves as being the original Americans because it would not coincide with the version of history that was crafted for us.

In 1865 the 13th Amendment of the Constitution was ratified to supposedly free the slaves; that year was also the beginning of the 'Reconstruction Era' of American history. It was a time for the country to rebuild after war, at that time the history of the land was reconstructed as well. That's when it became HIS-story.

"…they manipulate our history books, the history books are not true, it's a lie. The history books are lying. You need to know that. You must know that…"

~ Michael Jackson

9

The Atlantic, the Great Mirror

Thre are many similarities between Africa and America. Believe it or not, some scholars suggest that America is the original and things were later perfected in Africa.

We should recognize that our people were on both sides of the Ocean for thousands of years. Also remember Pangea, when the continents were not separate like they are today. Regardless of what came first, the similarities between the continents are undeniable.

The old man Mississippi River is sometimes called the Nile of the West, referencing the infamous Nile River in Africa; they are two of the largest rivers in the world.

There is a Great Lakes region in the middle of

North America, and there is also a Great Lakes region in the middle of Africa.

In Egypt, there are cities called **Cairo** and **Memphis** right along the Nile River. In America, there's a **Cairo** and **Memphis** right along the Mississippi River.

There was a tribe called the **Ben Isma-El Tribe** who was a nomadic tribe of American Indians or Moors, they moved throughout parts of Indiana and Illinois. They migrated in a triangular pattern that mimicked the shape the great pyramids. The tribe settled in between cities named **Mahomet**, **Mecca**, **Morocco**, and Cairo. Who knew that the midwestern part of the US had cities with those names?

The pyramids in Mexico, while not taller, are actually larger in capacity than the ones in Egypt. If both structures were turned upside down, the pyramids in Mexico would hold as much as four times more water, that gives you an idea of the size. The monuments in the Americas are a part of our legacy in this part of the world.

Many great, ancient "black" cultures were here just like they were in Africa. We aren't educated about these things on purpose. Great lengths were taken to make us think that we're not at home on this side of the Atlantic, but it's just not true.

The challenge we face today is letting go of and unlearning the "facts" that we've been inundated with for so long. This is hard for our people to do under-standably, it was hard for me as well. At some point, you have to question everything. Scrutinize this book too! I hope this information prompts you to do some searching of your own.

I often remind myself that in the Matrix, they generally didn't free a person's mind after a certain age. It was already too late at some point. They were in so deep that the brain would not let go of it. That can quite often be the case with us in this Matrix (USA) as well.

"I had seen ancient records that unveiled the world most explosive secret. 'Egypt' had crossed the Atlantic Sea, in ships, more than 10,000 years before the time of Christ. They had built the world's largest cities, in South and Central America, and in Mexico, and into Africa. I had broken the seal on the '*forbidden histories.*' I had found the writings that told how Egypt had built its most powerful empire, and it happened to be in the Americas.

...More disturbing to some, I had gotten the old maps that showed where the ancient Egyptian cities had stood, in the Americas.

...Ancient Egyptians had named the capital city 'HERU,' to keep alive the name of one of Egypt's founding kings. The city Heru was eventually called

Heru-Salem, then Jeru-Salem, and it had stood in the Americas. It was the presence of Jerusalem, in the Americas, that kept scholars quiet and preachers fearful, when I showed them the old maps and the ancient writings…and the *forbidden histories*"

An excerpt from: "**When Rocks Cry Out**"
by Horace Butler

10

It's Legal, Not Emotional

This is the most important thing you need to understand in this book, by **being classified as a black person, you do not have any standing in law**. That is a fact. And it does not matter how much you love being black and love your people.

I love my colorful, loud, crazy acting and lovely black people too! There's nothing like being at a concert or festival full of our people.

It's perfectly ok to identify with black casually. It's a normal part of conversation and acceptable socially. However **legally**, we cannot define ourselves as black people. This is something that we have to come to grips with.

People do not come in colors like crayons. People

belong to nations and have nationalities. There's no such thing as a black or white person!

Even black people ain't even black. We are a myriad of beautiful shades of brown (copper).

The light skin vs. dark skin thing just creates more division in an already fictitious category. Skin color doesn't even matter or mean anything. The system has dumbed down our pineal glands and simplified our thought processes so much, that we can be separated over anything. We've lost touch with our true nature and spirit.

We so-called black people are quick to call anyone who doesn't look like us white, but they are not white people. If pressed, people know their ancestry and can tell you that they are Polish, Irish, or German—whatever the case may be. They don't just take pride in or claim to be a color.

As 'black' people, we don't have any nationality. There is no country called Blackland. You might think what about African-American? Well, the continent of Africa has well over fifty different nations. A person from Africa would not stop just at the continent when describing their home. They name the specific country and region of Africa they are from, like **Nigerian**, **Lebanese**, or **Kenyan**. They don't just generically say that they are African.

Most Americans are uneducated when it comes to nationality because we're so used to referring to people as black or white.

You notice how we will say we're going 'to the Africans' to get our hair braided? Not to the Nigerians or whatever nation may apply. And we don't say it like they are our people either. If we are African-Americans, why do we say 'the Africans' as if they are not us? We clearly don't identify as that.

Please don't take this the wrong way, but from a legal perspective, it's ignorant to embrace black or African-American.

We were born amid a paper genocide that is still taking place right now in the United States of America. We find ourselves losing the game to the system that we don't even realize that we're playing.

The damage is being done to us via contracts, codes, and classifications. They made us into a new category of people on paper. Then new Amendments, statutes, and laws were created to govern the new people, who are actually considered less than people. We lack a proper name, status, and nationality. That is where they get the 3/5's of a man from.

Get a copy of the Constitution of the United States, the Constitution of your specific state, and a

Black's Law Dictionary. Keep them around for reference. If you are going to live in America, it behooves you to learn how the law operates.

11

It Matters What You Call Yourself!

I would strongly suggest that you consider some of the information in this book and do some research of your own. Draw your own conclusion from what resonates with you. Listen to the voice of your ancestors inside you.

Yes. It matters! I can almost hear people thinking, what difference does it make? Who cares? Why should I have to put any thought into what name you are called and classified as?

It's essential as a matter of truth, understanding, education, legality, and honor to our ancestors. We need to equip our youth with the facts to help us ultimately shift our people's overall mindset. As a people, we are lost in large part because we genuinely don't know who we are. We've accepted a false idea of ourselves.

Understanding of self is something that can build integrity inside of our youth. Armed with real knowledge we can help to restore us to the honor we've once known all over the world. That might be the thing that can make young men pull their pants up and resume our position as the original kings and queens of this land, moreover, this planet.

Knowledge is power. So, it definitely matters who we are. It does affect us. There are a few main things that our people absolutely need to know and understand:

* We so-called **'black' people are native to the Americas.** We did not all get brought here.

* When we classified ourselves as black people, it makes us second class citizens legally. It's not just social biases or racism, **by LAW a black person is a second class citizen**, **not a real American Citizen.** It's written precisely that way.

* His-story, as taught to us, **is made up of lies and fabrications.**

We cannot continue to ignore the legality that lies behind our current situation in America. Our legal status is the underlying factor to mistreatment of our people. That is what we need to address collectively.

Nothing is going to change until we address that. We can complain about racism or police brutality, but it will not produce any results.

It's time that we move more wisely and understand the structure of how this system is put together. Remember, ignorance of the law is no excuse.

Don't think for a second that i"s in any way beyond our understanding. If you just open yourself to learning, then the information you seek will come to you. Use this book as a starting point to discover some brand new things.

12

Black Lives Actually Don't Matter!

We take pride in being black. Black Americans are a new tribe is the way one of my best friend describes it. I get that. We have an emotional attachment to the name. As a *social* term, referring to ourselves as black is fine, but as a ***legal*** term its a huge detriment and the law is unforgiving. So we so-called black people need to approach things legally and not emotionally.

How is a black person seen in the eyes of the law? The answer is **Civiliter Mortuus**. That is a latin legal term that means: **Civilly dead; dead in the view of the law. The condition of one who has lost his civil rights and capacities, and is accounted dead in law.**

That's the underlying reason why the police can

beat, shoot, or kill black people and never get prosecuted. Because blacks have no legal standing to begin with. That's what enables and empowers the systematic racism we see in America. We think that it's because of the color of our skin, but that has nothing to do with it.

Our protests in the past were about fighting for our civil rights, but it was basic human rights that we lacked and still do not possess. They love to see us pray or march for change because it will never result in us addressing the heart of the issue, which is our classification and legal status.

First, there exists no nation of 'Black Americans' nor is there a 'Black America' in any documented record, the world over! Black Americans are what is referred to in Law as a 'misnomer', or collectively, misnomers. As you well know, grammatically, 'black' is an *adjective* and is not a *proper noun*. Socially and politically, 'black' implies '*Civiliter Mortuus*', which means '*Dead in the eyes of Law*'. Black American is not a Nationality nor is it a Nation; therefore 'black' has no political interests nor powers in the Free National Constitution that was prepared for all Free National Beings.

13

Be Wary of Our Leaders

The information in that last chapter is not top secret. Anyone who studies basic civics or examines the Constitution of the United States would begin to know and understand that.

Years ago this kind of thing was not public knowledge, but today we live in an age of abundant information. So why would any conscious leaders and scholars continue to refer to us as 'black' people? Talking about black pride but failing even to mention how much it can hinder us as a nationality is a red flag. Either they are not aware or they're purposely not enlightening our people.

You have to watch some of these clowns, they could very well be agents working for the other side to keep our people entertained, distracted, and stuck in this legally dead status. The system has historically used the popular black artist, entertainers, pastors, and community leaders as pawns to help keep the people ignorant.

Back in the day, it was a contrived plan to get our people to embrace being "black and proud," because they knew it would covertly keep us dead in the eyes of the law. The more we embrace new labels for ourselves, the further we separate ourselves from our historical legacy.

A race is nothing more than a social construct used as a distraction. There's only one race of people, the human race. The powers that be love when we expend all of our energies on the frustrations of racism, "the white man," or the ridiculous American political landscape. Those things only divert our attention from the real issues of legal standing.

Platforms are easy to build today. Lecturers give themselves nicknames, create egotistical titles, and use entertaining language—but very few of them talk about the thing that really matters. A true leader assumes the responsibility of teaching the people the truth at all cost. Hold them to that. Ask them about Civiliter Mortuus and why they are still calling us black people.

Two of our most popular and respected leaders, Dr. Martin Luther King and Malcolm X were aware. They knew that America is our homeland and they both spoke about it before their assassinations. Both of them had also began talking about our people controlling our own economics towards the end of their lives.

In honor of them and the many other men and women who've fought for our people, we have to carry that torch forward. We have access to so much more information and different platforms to link up and do business today.

"...the Negro finds himself in exile in his own land..."

~ Dr. Martin Luther King Jr.

"…we didn't land on Plymouth Rock, the rock was landed on us…"

~ Malcolm X

14

Officially Changing Your Status

H ere is where things can get very tricky. Untangling ourselves from the web of the system can prove to be a tedious task.

We are all contracted into the system by way of birth certificate, driver's license, etc. Correcting those contracts and your status is the only real way to be free of the Matrix system that is America.

Some people have made a scam of selling people 'sovereignty' paperwork packages. Anyone that's making promises to you that sound too good to be true are most likely not. Study things for yourself. Correcting our status is not a get rich quick scheme or some plot for you to make money. It's about proclaiming yourself a free, national Citizen of America, as opposed to a citizen of the United States of

America. Look into all avenues and see what resonates with you.

It is well within anyone's legal rights to correct their legal classification and/or nationality. We can claim whatever we think our true nationality is for the record. This has to be done correctly as any error will make your claim invalid, and subsequently, your legal status will remain the same.

The key is proving a pre-colonial connection to America. In other words, we are saying that we have ancestry with bloodlines from the Americas that predates the colonies. The US was only founded in 1776, the original people of this land have tribes and treaties that predate the existence of the United States. The majority if not all the so-called black people fit into that category, we just have to prove and declare it.

Be clear that this system does not want to lose people and tax dollars. At all. In fact, if they catch people making errant mistakes, they will seek to punish and humiliate them. They want to dissuade people from even trying to challenge the system.

Moor and more people are waking up to the fact that we are not all from Africa. The system is well aware of this fact too. The FBI has a new group of what they label as domestic terrorist called **Black**

Identity Extremist. They are using that to harass any groupings of people of color who are making too much noise about building a nation or just escaping the system of the United States. If too many people learn the truth, then the whole system will crash.

So we must be move wisely inside the United States of America and be especially meticulous if trying to escape it on paper. Mentally freeing yourself is a mandatory first step. The more that you learn, the easier that will become.

The stuff chapter may sound really extreme to many people reading this, but it's really not. Once you begin to understand the trickery of this system, it will become clear why you don't want to participate in it. There's a big game being played.

Even if making an official declaration is too much for you personally, we should not discount the value in honoring your ancestors by finding out who you indeed are and claiming it out loud.

Think of your children and the future generations of your family, they deserve to know their truth. Don't pass down a tradition of them calling themselves colors. Talk with and record the elders in your family. The National Archives of every state keeps all birth, death, and marriage records—you can find out information on your family history there. Ancestry.com is a legit source for searches too, it can help you find and identify members of your family. (Those DNA tests, however, are merely a hoax in my opinion. Don't ha)

We don't discuss our own family's history enough with the youth. Basically, all 'black' folks in America have roots somewhere in the south right? Our elders often know of "Indian" branches of the family, but it's not discussed enough. My mom blurted out to me recently when I was talking to her, "...oh, your grandfather Walter Hayes was a tall, handsome, regal man; people would always say he looked Indian, he had those high cheekbones and carried himself like royalty."

Those conversations need to be had in all our families before we lose the sources. Now I want to go check for his birth records and any census forms he was included on in Mississippi. She gave me his wife's name too. I can search for their parents and follow that trail as far back as possible. You'll find that exploring your family history is both an interesting and fulfilling quest.

15

Let's Agree Enough to Circulate the "Black" Dollars!

C urrent reports state that a dollar circulates for a month in Asian communities, in the Jewish community its seventeen days. Twenty-one times in their community before leaving. In the black community, a dollar lasts just HOURS. The "black" dollar is circulating *zero* times in our own communities! Our money goes directly to someone doesn't look like us. That is a tragedy, it's the major problem that we face as a people.

In order to correct this and start working together to change it immediately, regardless of our creed. We are crippled financially and nothing else matters until we fix that problem first.

I love all the brothers and sisters on Youtube

lecturing. I want to start a channel myself. I've watched all the endless debates in the community regarding **nationality**, **Christianity**, **Islam**, **Pan-Africanism**, **Moorish science**, **Hebrew Israelites** and all of it. A lot of good information was spread, but at the same time, it's still not helping to solve our economic status at all. All of us are not going to agree. We just have to be ok with that.

In the big picture there's no need to argue right now. Our top priority should be building an economic base in our community, before deciphering the details of the past. The energy (currency) is racing out of our community bleeding us dry.

We are creative people, make and sell something. You can have a different ideology than your brothers or sisters and still do business with them! **You don't have to be a Muslim to buy a bean pie.** Start finding ways to routinely do business with people that look like you. Teach your family the value in that.

In fact, that's an excellent way to honor and represent the aspect of culture that you embrace. Doing good business with people promotes your philosophy without words.

Too many of our intelligent teachers become egotistical and tainted. It sadly seems as though scandals and scams consistently accompany their popularity. At times it feels like the whole conscious community is slowly becoming a new version of church, peddling feel-good speeches (or videos), full of empty promises, but never actually creating any change.

Humbling ourselves and working together is the only way to strengthen the community. With tools like social media at our disposal today, there are ample opportunities to organize together. Think in terms of being a producer and not just a consumer.

In some ways, it's actually a good thing that there's no one to follow. We should not idolize any one man or woman, we should instead look inside of ourselves for a leader. The voice of our ancestors is screaming inside of us already. Quiet the outer world and travel inside of your own universe sometimes for balance.

As far as your perspective on nationality, gravitate towards with what resonates with you. Just make sure you pick for yourself. In the end, it's possible that we are all right in one way or another. People feel and are drawn to different things for different reasons. We should always follow our spirit and honor our ancestors. All we can do is present our perspective on knowledge and build with those people who connect with it.

In the meantime, let's do and create businesses with each other. We can still debate after that.

16

So What Should We Call Ourselves?

No one can answer that question for you. You have to honor yourself. This book is imploring you to not accept the labels that were given to us.

Many people have a family connection to a specific Native American tribe. Even if you don't know any tribal history, you should know that you are an aboriginal. Remember the old common saying about having good hair ~ 'oh, you got some Indian in your family?' *Everybody* used to say that without realizing how correct true those words were.

Let's use my family members for an example, as far as I know, we've always considered ourselves regular black folks or African-Americans. Living in the city for some time, but from down south, like the average black family.

Most people of color in America refer to ourselves as black and check the African-American box on forms. That is a routine that we all have to get out of. It matters. And it's not true, we are not African-American.

Like many families in the midwest, mine comes from Mississippi. Looking at our family matriarch, Emma Beard (pictured below, with her daughter, my Nana, aunt Phyllis, one of her nine children), she clearly has what would be called Native American features, the complexion, and hair. Most of my family have native features. Then again, whatever features we have are native, because we are the native people.

Just looking at my beautiful Granny and Aunt, most people would agree that they look closer to what we would call "Indian," than they look "African."

Another one of her children was my late uncle Art, (next page), was a big, strong man with a huge presence; he had a big head that was similar to the great Olmec heads found in Mexico. He had a barrel chest, broad shoulders, and a huge booming voice of a pastor. My friend used to joke that when he sneezed, it would shake the whole house. He was a great leader of our family and exemplified the strength of our ancestors. I wonder if he ever even knew about the Olmec heads at all. Knowledge was much harder to come by in those days. I wish I had been interested in all of this while he and my dad were alive.

If you're lucky enough to have elders in your family, share this information with them. Talk with them about your family history, and you may be surprised how much you can learn. Ask about your relatives down south. We have always been taught that they separated us from our home and culture, but it was actually hidden from us, right under our feet. Talk with your parents and grandparents while you can. Even if your elders have transitioned and are now ancestors, ask them to guide you to the information you seek.

We wouldn't just call ourselves the generic term 'Indian.' As an aside, even people from India were not called Indians historically. The country was called Hindustan (or Bharat), and the people were Hindu. Because of the brainwashing of the public school (fool) system, the terms Native American, American Indian and Indian are forever linked in our heads and vocabulary.

Judging by the looks alone, it's safe to say that my

family definitely has some so-called Indian ancestry. So we could more accurately refer to ourselves as **American Indians**. That is exponentially better than calling ourselves a color (black), or the hyphenated name (African-American). And it is true. It's legit. Don't think you're just saying it to have something to say. No. We are the true natives of this land. Don't let the deceptive version of history or false imagery the system has impressed on us make you think differently.

American aboriginal is an even more accurate term. It means that we are the original inhabitants of this land. We so-called black people are aboriginal all over the planet, the great pan-African professor Dr. James Smalls even confirms that. We have to embrace that knowledge of ourselves out loud in America. We cannot continue to use whatever name or label they want to give to us.

In the next few sections, we'll explore a few options about what we can call ourselves. Some of these have caused some heated debates among the YouTube scholars and the community at large. Do some exploring of these on your own and gravitate towards what resonates with you.

Think for yourself and draw your own conclusions, that's the idea of this whole book. In fact, you can draw your own box. On a form that's asking your nationality, you're NOT limited to the choices that are offered. You can make your own box and write the name that you deem is appropriate for yourself. Always remember that.

17

Meditate On It

Don't be afraid to ask questions to your ancestors even after they have passed on, ask them to reveal themselves to you. Take a moment before bed to ask questions and listen to your dreams. I have had the ancestors communicate with me in the dream world for sure. I'm still interpreting some of them.

In one memorable dream, I was wandering in a place far away from the city, through some vast, open plains. These two big men who seemed liked guardians rode up to me on big horses. They looked very similar to the man in the Moorish Chief painting (page 89).

Both of them had on jeweled breastplates and had weapons, like mighty warriors. They were in total command of the giant horses that stood perfectly still as they focused on me. Their presence was imposing. One of them asked me about what I was doing around there. I told him I was just looking around, seeking to learn more about where I came from.

They looked at each other and smirked, tacitly confirming that I was no threat.

Then one of them looked down at me and stared right into my eyes, asking me in a deep voice, "**What kind of Indians come from Kentucky?**"

I thought hard about it, but I had no idea. I shrugged my shoulders. They could see that I didn't know too much. I felt ashamed, as though I should've at least known that much. They gave me a farewell nod before riding off into the sunset kicking up a trail of dust.

It was one of those very realistic dreams, and my dad is actually from Louisville. It gave me a point of reference and a place to continue my research.

18

Autochthon American People Nation

The Autochthon American People Nation is an American aboriginal government Nation. It's not a 501c3. As is states on their website, "We are not federally recognized and we do not wish to be. As the original people of this landmass called the Americas/Turtle Island and her surroundings, we have the right to belong to a Nation and not be forced to assimilate to other people's culture, ways, practices, ideologies etc."

This is something that you might want to look into. A nation of people that are all about our people reclaiming our identity in our homeland. In this case if asked your nationality, you could simply say American, say the whole thing. Investigate this nation for yourself, if nothing else its an opportunity to learn something. I had only recently learned about it, and I think there is a lot to love about it.

Here is one more thing off the website, autochthonapn.com, that makes a whole lot of sense: "We are not a Patriarchal or Matriarchal Nation/Tribe/Family who believe in balance since both masculine and feminine exist in the Great I AM/Great Spirit. We do not believe any one man or woman should rule over another, but instead we believe we were created to compliment each other... Many are called but the chosen are few, and the chosen can be either male, female, or both; that should lead the people in truth, love, harmony and light always."

This is something I want to learn much more about.

Luzia

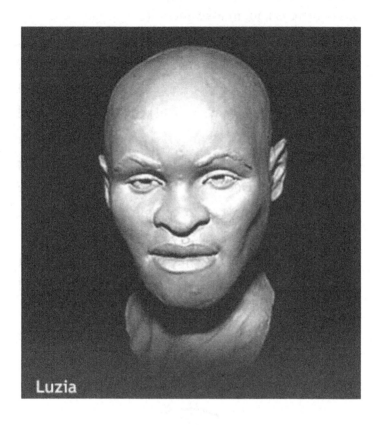

Luzia

Luzia is the recreation of the oldest human ever found in the Americas. The remains were discovered in 1975 and archeologist say that the remains are over 12,000 years old. She was given the name Luzia in homage to "Lucy," the famous 3.2 million-year-old remains found in Africa. That means 'black' people have been here for three million damn years! How could Europeans claim to have discovered anything?

Luzia was one of the most prized possessions of the National Museum of Brazil in Rio de Janeiro. The museum was destroyed by a massive fire in 2018, the Luzia remains were partially recovered from the debris.

So back in 1975, there was undeniable proof of a "black" lady in the Americas some 12,000 years ago. In 1990, the full remains of a 5,000-year-old pyramid civilization (City of Coral), was verified in Peru. How do they still teach the same Pilgrim and Indian story to us?

Why do we continue to accept the blatant lies? We can't allow them to program our children's minds with rhetoric. When are we finally going to wake up and reject it?

19

The Aboriginal Movement

D ane Calloway does a great job researching and presenting historical data. His work debunks the notion that everyone black is from Africa. He teaches that we are the true native Americans. Not to take his word for it, Calloway encourages us to trace our own family histories and we will see for ourselves that we are indeed Aboriginals and most of us did not arrive on a boat. He presents his material in a very easy-to-follow manner.

All of the great authors, scholars, and teachers of the community deserve credit, **especially the elders who were doing the work before YouTube even existed**. Much respect to all of them.

Tasha Xi is another independent researcher who focuses our indigenous history. Turtle Gang makes some dope documentaries and is very knowledgable about his own genealogy. She documents her visits to the Library of Congress and presents lots of extremely valuable information as well. Be sure to support her efforts.

Kurimeo Ahau's documentaries are incredible too, he's put together some powerful stuff. Check out his work and support his effort.

Aseer The Duke of Tiers is very clear and knowledgeable giving a Moorish perspective of history. Check out his videos and support his work as well.

The Federation of Aboriginal Nations of the Americas, is a federation of as many as a dozen different nations of American aboriginals. The FADA director, General Neesu Wushuwunoag, is a very knowledgable brother and he puts out thought provoking information out on YouTube.

For more historical information on the Moundbuilders check out the work of <u>Dr. R. A. Umar Shabazz Bey</u>.

20

New Era Detroit

New Era Detroit is an activist group who is all about taking action in the community. N.E.D. is the most productive and organized group in the 'black' community since the Black Panthers.

The group has expanded and now there are chapters of New Era in Cleveland, Chicago, and Miami. The focus of the group is to harness the enormous economic power the black dollar, something that we desperately need in our communities.

From their website (neweradetroit.com), it states: (NED) and its chapters plan on using those resources, (black) money, and that power to take back our communities and start up a SOLELY BLACK-OWNED COMMUNITY. We're aiming to create Black owned and operated schools, banks, grocery stores, hospitals, law offices, recreation centers, and more!

The best thing about this group is that they take it to the streets for real! They have shut down liquor stores, gas stations, and checked churches for disrespecting the community. N.E.D. supports and promotes black-owned businesses constantly, putting action behind their words. They deserve respect for that.

I encourage people to look into and if inclined donate to this organization and support their efforts. Instead of financing YouTube scholars who are just talking history, donate to people who are in the streets getting stuff done. Reach out to them about starting a chapter in your city.

They talk about 'black power,' but I hope this book reaches them so they can understand the legal issues associated with being legally classified as blacks/African-Americans. Addressing the paperwork status could just be the domino that gives our people true power and sovereignty.

21

Moors

The Moors are most known in history for ruling in Spain and throughout early Europe. From 742 AD up until the fall of the Grenada in 1492, Spain was under Moorish rule.

Left out of history is the assertion that the Americas, (aka **Turtle Island, Al-Moroc or Northwest/Southwest Amexem**), was also home to a Moorish empire.

The story of Estivanico (Chapter 24), is very revealing. It says that once he reached Mexico, that he was reunited with his countrymen. He was a Moor. So that's a clear indication that Moors or "black" people were residing in Mexico (America) at that time.

'Black' people today truly don't have an understanding of Moors. Some people even separate the

Moors from the great cultures of Egypt, or Africa, and early America, but we are all the same people. If there were no labels or names given to the people, just photos, we would see that we're the same people throughout the history of the world. The names cause a separation. Dr. James Smalls teaches that the Moors were charged with being the custodians of Kemetic culture.

The oldest existing treaty in the world is the Treaty of Peace and Friendship between the United States of America and Morocco. The treaty is still ratified every fifty years. The country of Morocco where we know it today was established in 1956; the treaty is from 1787, so where was Morocco at that time?

The Moroccan flag is the oldest flag on earth, it's over 10,000 years old. The five pointed, interlocking star on the flag represents Love, truth, peace, freedom, and justice. Many scholars say that the George Washington chopping down the cherry tree was a metaphor for Europeans chopping down of the Moorish flag.

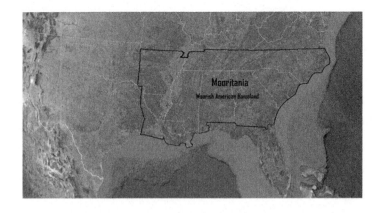

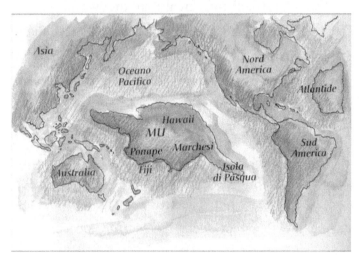

Throughout history and among different languages, there are tons of variations and spellings of the word Moor. (Mohr, Morisco, Mauro, Morris, Mauri, etc.). Mu, was one of the oldest variations that derived from a continent that no longer exist, **Mu** or **Lumuria**. The people there were called Mu'urs.

The most enlightening part of studying Moorish Science is obtaining an understanding of law. Moors teach about mastering the language of law and grasping the foundation of how this corporate United States came into existence. We all need to be aware of contracts, jurisdiction, and legal status because those are the things that allow for the mistreatment that is often mislabeled as racism to take place.

22

The Mound Builders

The **Washitaw Muurs** in Louisiana is one of the oldest recorded civilizations in history. The Washitaw, (and the Olmecs), were known as the Mound Builders. There were as many as 200,000 mounds in the Americas, half of them are still standing. In the United States, most mounds are found all along the Mississippi River and in the midwest. The mounds were built all over the Americas, from Alaska to Peru.

The area of Southern Illinois is still till today known as "little Egypt." Near the city Cairo, IL, theres a town called Mounds and another one called Mound City.

Many mound structures were destroyed and some remain hidden away from the public in private golf courses and country clubs. In Ohio, there is the infamous Mound of the Serpent that is an incredible 1.5 miles long; it's symbolically shaped like a snake swallowing an egg or the sun. During the summer solstice the snake's head is perfectly aligned with the sunset. The same type of astrologically based architecture found in all the pyramids of the world. Built by the same people.

Monks Mound is located a mile from the Mississippi river, just north of East St. Louis, Illinois. This amazing mound consists of more than **two billion pounds** of non-local soil types. It's an amazing structure considering the time that it was built, it was constructed to be timeless. The base of Monk's Mound is actually bigger than the base of the great pyramid and covers over fourteen acres of land. That astounding land structure is a part of our ancestry that still stands right in the middle of the country, and most of us don't even know about it. I certainly didn't. What a great summer road trip destination.

In that same region of Illinois, **Burrow's Cave** was discovered along the river. It had many artifacts that could only be described as "African." How did those things get there? Archeologists have no tangible explanation for the findings. It all confirms the inevitable truth that black people had been here long ago.

Many people say that it was American Indians, specifically the **Choctaw Indian Tribe**, who are the Mound Builders. And ultimately perhaps everyone is right. What we can agree on is that the mounds are ancient structures, and the people who built them look like what we would all call black folks today. That's the bottom line, no matter what name they went by.

Why don't American history classes say anything about this? It's obvious that the decision to suppress this knowledge is because it would not work with their narrative.

Serpents Mound, Ohio

Monk's Mound, Illinois

23

Blackamoor

Before the word nigger there was another derogatory word used to describe us so-called black people, it was **blackamoor**. In the dictionary it reads as follows:

blackamoor

noun, *Older Use: Disparaging and Offensive.*

1. a contemptuous term used to refer to a black person.
2. a contemptuous term used to refer to <u>any dark-skinned person.</u>

First recorded in 1540-50; **unexplained variant of phrase *black Moor.*** It says that blackamoor was used to describe any dark-skinned person, it's a variant of the term black Moor. So that's a definitive clue that people of color at that time were known as Moors. The term Moor is already synonymous with darker skin people, but **it does not mean 'black'** as many scholars say. Blackamoor wouldn't make sense then, it would be saying someone "black-a-black."

According to the etymology, this derogatory term blackamoor originated in 1540-1550, around fifty years after the arrival of Columbus.

We know about the dominant Moorish presence in Spain and Europe for many centuries, but Moors also brought medicine and civilization all over the world. America (Al-Moroc), once had a strong Moorish presence as well. Both the term blackamoor and the story of Estivanico (Chapter 24) support that theory.

Morocco is in northern part of the continent of Africa today. When someone begins to take pride in their Moorish heritage, people sometimes mistake it as a diss to Africa or more recently, to the Aboriginal American movement.

Nobody is disparaging Africa, it just seems as if all of our people's pride invested only there. It's important that we understand that we are at home right here too; we are not displaced! No matter what you call yourself, that fact needs to be thoroughly understood.

All black people were not brought to this land, our ancestors travelled to and traded on this land for thousands of years. That is a fact. Someone came and swindled our land from us, redefined everything, and told us we were from far, far away. History gives a false impression that America was 'new land' and not an ancient land that was already civilized many times over. People are just beginning to learn the truth.

"...We were here in this land (known as) the United States of America **before Europeans ever came into existence**."

~ Michael Imhotep

24

Moorish Chief

The infamous Moorish Chief painting is a very popular piece of art. It was in several of my family members' homes.

That picture is hanging in my mom's living room right now. She said that she's had it for quite a while and didn't remember where she got it from. I might have seen it growing up, but I don't remember it. There's also one in my uncle Arthur's household where I spent a lot of time as a youth. I didn't really pay much attention to it at that time, not consciously at least.

I still notice it frequently in random places. It's a welcomed contrast to the ubiquitous picture of the white Jesus that I used to cringe at in people's homes.

I wonder if folks realize that it's a Moorish painting. I assume that many people think it's just a regal black guy. The painting definitely captures the class, power, and royalty of the Moorish chief. I hope that we can realize those qualities inside of ourselves as well.

25

Estevanico the Moor

"As long as the concept of an African-American is current and as long as African-American history is seen as beginning with enslavement in Africa, then Estaban is important because he is the first African-American."

~ Robert Goodwin, historian and author,
"Crossing the Continent, 1527-1540, The
Story of the first African-American
Explorer of the American South"

According to Goodwin, and other historic accounts, Estevanico was the first known person born in Africa to have arrived in the present day United States. The story is very interesting, especially in regards to the way that the great explorer was described.

He went by many different names in different languages. He was called "Mustafa Zemmouri," "Black Stephen," "Esteban," "Esteban the Moor," Estebanico, Stephen the Black, Stephen the Moor, Estevan, Stephen Dorantes, and "Little Stephen."

That's a lot of names. It most notable to me that he was a known Moor. He was said to be enslaved as a youth by the Portuguese, he was sold to a Spanish nobleman and taken in 1527 on the Spanish Narvaez expedition. He was then one of only four survivors in a journey from Cuba to the Florida coast.

After spending many years (some say in captivity), among Indian tribes, Estevanico escaped with the other three survivors and they went on a documented eight year expedition across the continent.

Estevanico was known to be a powerful healer who had great knowledge of herbs and natural remedies. Obviously a very intelligent man, he was also said to be a polyglot, who could learn the languages of native tribes very quickly.

I was fascinated by this story. Although it seems fairly common, I had never heard about it at all until I was researching for this book in 2019.

In the story so many of the terms used to describe so-called black people—Moor, black, Indian and negro—are used somewhat interchangeably.

Esteban was from Morocco, by way of Spain and therefore he was African. He was a Moor, (which should help end the debate about Moors being African or not). He travelled among, interacted, and lived so fluently with the native tribes probably because they resembled one another already.

The very end of his story is the most enlightening part. When Esteban found his way to modern day Mexico, it's where it says he was united with his countrymen again. That means that Mexico must have been a Moorish or "black" territory at that time.

Taking the whole tale into account, should confirm for us all that people who look like us were established here for many centuries, long before his-story teaches us.

It's way past time for us to redefine his-story!

Moorish presence is prominent all over the world. The book *Nature Knows No Color Lines* clearly illustrates that. George Washington was often pictured with sharply dressed Moorish brothers, sometimes in turbans. They are often captioned as "slaves," but always looked regal and were most likely teaching Washington our sciences. Even the Catholic Pope (page 94), has a Moorish ('black') Goddess in a crown looming over his head still till this day.

References

These are a few of the books/authors that have influenced my work, they make great points of reference. In a broader sense this book is a culmination of a lifetime of (re)searching and comes from innumerable sources (and spirits). Perusing the works of any of the scholars mentioned (or quoted) in the text is a perfect place to start to uncover things on your own.

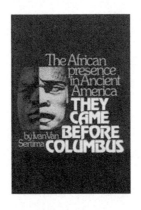

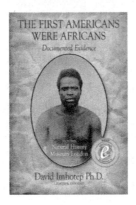

Acknowledgments

I give thanks to my ancestors for continuing to watch over me and my family. I want to thank the universe for showing me so many things to learn and share; I love this is part of my path.

Big thanks to all the scholars, lecturers, authors, historians, friends, podcasters, bloggers, professors, and other people that I've gained knowledge from along my life's journey; there are far too many to list, but all are appreciated. Keep up the good work.

Thank you Mom for being everything; I love you. Lastly thank you all for reading, considering, and sharing this information. Look out for new and upcoming releases from **Ra One Publications.**

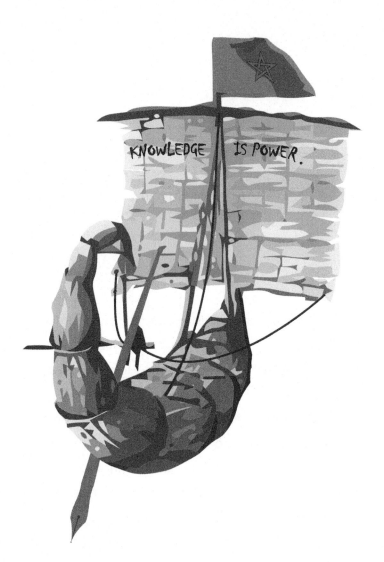

About the Author

Ray Stone has been working in urban health & wellness for over a decade. Life changed dramatically for the former Detroit Firefighter after a colon cleanse and subsequent switch to vegan diet & lifestyle. It opened his eyes on many levels.

Stone has since dedicated himself to learning and sharing spiritually inspired information to everyone within his reach. The author's strength lies in being able to relate to people of all backgrounds and communicate with them effectively. He currently has six titles available through his own company **Ra One Publications**.

www.ra1books.com
rstone.el@icloud.com

Also by Ray Stone

Check out other titles from Ra One Publications:

Personally, I will always love and prefer physical books. I was extremely late and reluctant to join the world of digital publishing. Now that I'm inevitably into it, I'm excited to take advantage of some of the amazing new interactive features available through digital publishing. The titles below are being reproduced and prepared for digital releases. We have a lot of great information to repackage and disseminate. Stay tuned.

Eat Like You Give A Damn: Beginning Your Lifestyle Transition By Ray Stone (2011)

Products of Our Environment By Ray Stone
(2014)

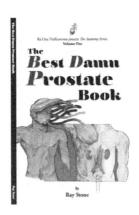

The Anatomy series volume I: **The Best Damn Prostate Book** By Ray Stone (2015)

The Anatomy series volume II: **iCare: Eye Health in the Technology** By Ray Stone (2019)

COMING SOON!

The Anatomy series volume III:

The Best Damn Yoni Book

By Ray Stone (2019-20)

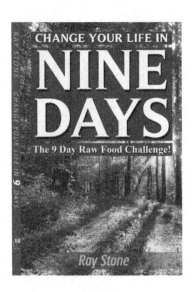

Change Your Life in Nine Days: The 9 Day Raw Food Challenge! By Ray Stone (2019)

An Easy Intro to Stones and Crystals by Ray Stone (2019)

COMING SOON!

Strictly for my Negus: The Strength of Street Knowledge

By Ray Stone (2019)

Made in the USA
Middletown, DE
20 February 2022

61484870R00070